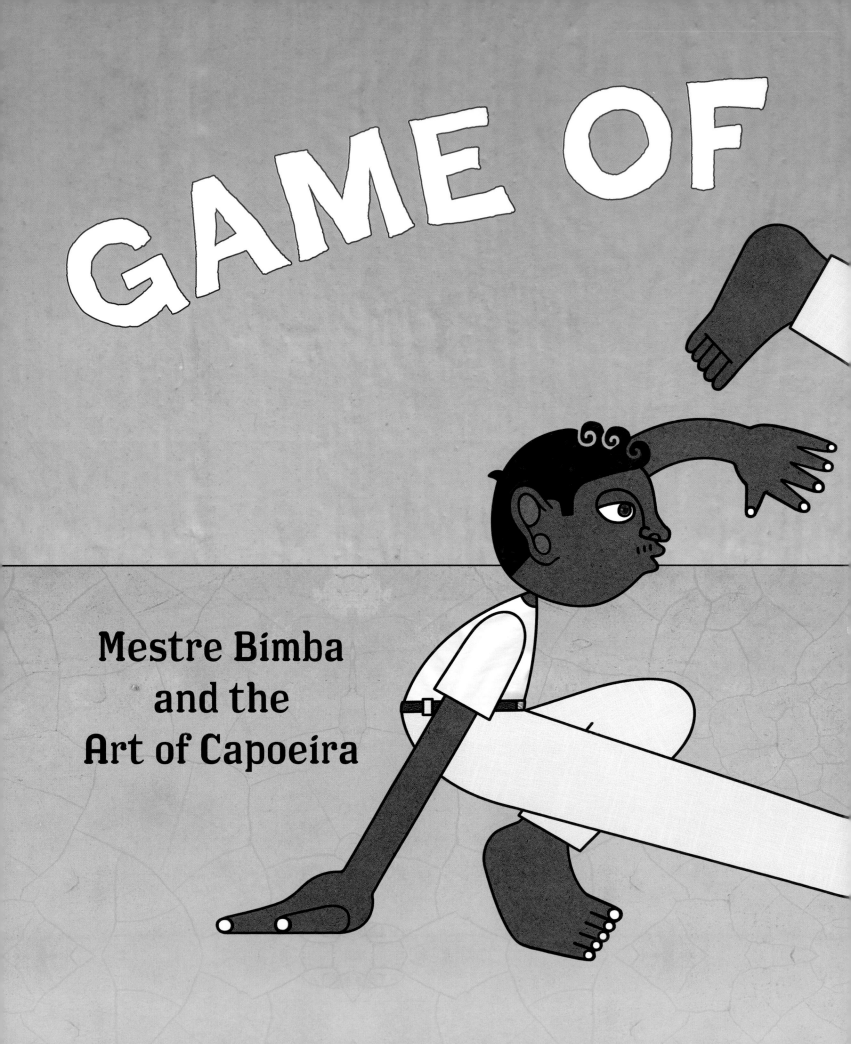

GAME OF

Mestre Bimba
and the
Art of Capoeira

FREEDOM

by
DUNCAN
TONATIUH

ABRAMS BOOKS FOR YOUNG READERS

NEW YORK

The illustrations in this book were hand-drawn and then collaged digitally.

A glossary and pronunciation guide for Portuguese words can be found in the back of the book.

Pages 40-41 photo credits: public domain; page 42 photo credit: cokada/iStock.com;
page 43 photo credit: FabioFilzi/iStock.com

Cataloging-in-Publication Data has been applied for and
may be obtained from the Library of Congress.

ISBN 978-1-4197-6458-5

Text and illustrations © 2023 Duncan Tonatiuh
Book design by Heather Kelly
Edited by Howard W. Reeves

Printed and bound in China
10 9 8 7 6 5 4 3 2 1

Abrams® is a registered trademark of Harry N. Abrams, Inc.

ABRAMS The Art of Books
195 Broadway, New York, NY 10007
abramsbooks.com

To my Longe do Mar friends. Axé!

Manoel ran down the cobblestoned streets. He could hear the sound of the berimbau playing in the distance. As he got closer, he could see a circle of people clapping and singing. A meia lua whooshed in the air. The strike was evaded and followed with an aú. Two young men were playing capoeira in the middle of the roda. Bimba (beam-bah), as everyone called Manoel, wanted to play too. He loved capoeira, with its kicks and acrobatic moves done to the rhythm of the music.

Bimba looked around. All the capoeiristas were Black men. In the early part of the twentieth century, most of the people in the city of Salvador and in the state of Bahia, where Bimba lived, were Black too. Like him, they were descendants of Africans who had been forced by the Portuguese to come to Brazil, their new colony, to work as slaves.

In the new land, the beliefs and customs that the enslaved people brought from their different African nations mixed and adapted to their new environment. Out of this mixture came new kinds of music, like samba. The combination also created new religions, like Candomblé. Another one of these cultural expressions was capoeira, which combined music, fighting, theatrics, and dance.

When Bimba was a teenager in the 1910s, the rich and powerful in
Salvador were predominantly white. They did not care about these
Black expressions. They often disdained them, especially capoeira,
which they thought was barbaric and practiced only by malandros.

Bimba was not surprised that, just as he was entering the roda, someone yelled, "The police are coming!" Everyone ran. It was illegal to play capoeira in the streets. The police beat up the capoeiristas they caught and threw them in jail. *They chase us like dogs*, Bimba thought as he scurried away.

Around the age of twelve, Bimba began working on the docks.
There, he learned to play capoeira from a ship captain. When he was
not at work, Bimba taught others. But as the years went on, he became
frustrated. A lot of people in Salvador did not respect capoeira.
He was tired of being chased every time he played the game.

Bimba decided to develop a new style of capoeira. He wanted to revolutionize the game and demonstrate that the jogo could be an effective martial art. He incorporated new movements into his style. Some were from batuque, a fighting game that his father practiced that was popular in Salvador. He called his new kind of capoeira Luta Regional Baiana, or "regional" for short.

In 1932, Bimba opened an academia to teach regional. He became a mestre, a teacher of the art. It was the first time capoeira was taught inside in a structured way. Until then, people had learned the game informally, mostly by watching others play in the street and imitating them.

Rules:
Wear a white uniform.
No smoking or drinking alcohol.
You must have a job or be in school.

Mestre Bimba wanted capoeira to lose its bad reputation. He established strict rules for those who wanted to become his pupils. It was not long before university students and doctors, who would normally snub the game, started taking classes at his school too. The formality and discipline, similar to those of other sports, appealed to them.

Mestre Bimba developed a teaching method for regional. The first movement students learned was the ginga, which means "to swing." Capoeira players are never static. They are constantly moving, and ginga is the fundamental step. "Capoeira doesn't exist without the ginga," Mestre Bimba would say.

After they had mastered the ginga, students learned sequences of movements that they practiced in pairs. Some movements were attacks, others were defenses, and yet others were takedowns. The mestre created these sequences so that students could quickly develop the necessary skills to play well.

Once students learned to perform the sequences, they were ready for their batizado and played in the roda with an advanced pupil to the rhythm of music and songs. After the rookies played, they received their nicknames from the mestre. Capoeiristas had the habit of using nicknames when they played in the street so that the police could not identify them easily.

Mestre Bimba held special graduation ceremonies for more experienced students. Guests attended these events. The pupils had to perform advanced movements, sing, and play capoeira according to different berimbau rhythms. Afterward, students received silk handkerchiefs to wear around their necks. The handkerchief's color depended on the student's level.

As he taught more and more pupils, Bimba decided it was time
to test his regional style with capoeiristas who did not train
with him. He began going to different rodas in the street.
Whenever Bimba and his students played, they dominated the
jogo with their cabeçadas and vingativas.

Capoeira players who were not familiar with the mestre were impressed with his skills and precise movements. Bimba became known as a great capoeirista throughout Salvador. But the mestre was not satisfied. He went to one of Bahia's major newspapers and put out a public challenge to all fighters in the city.

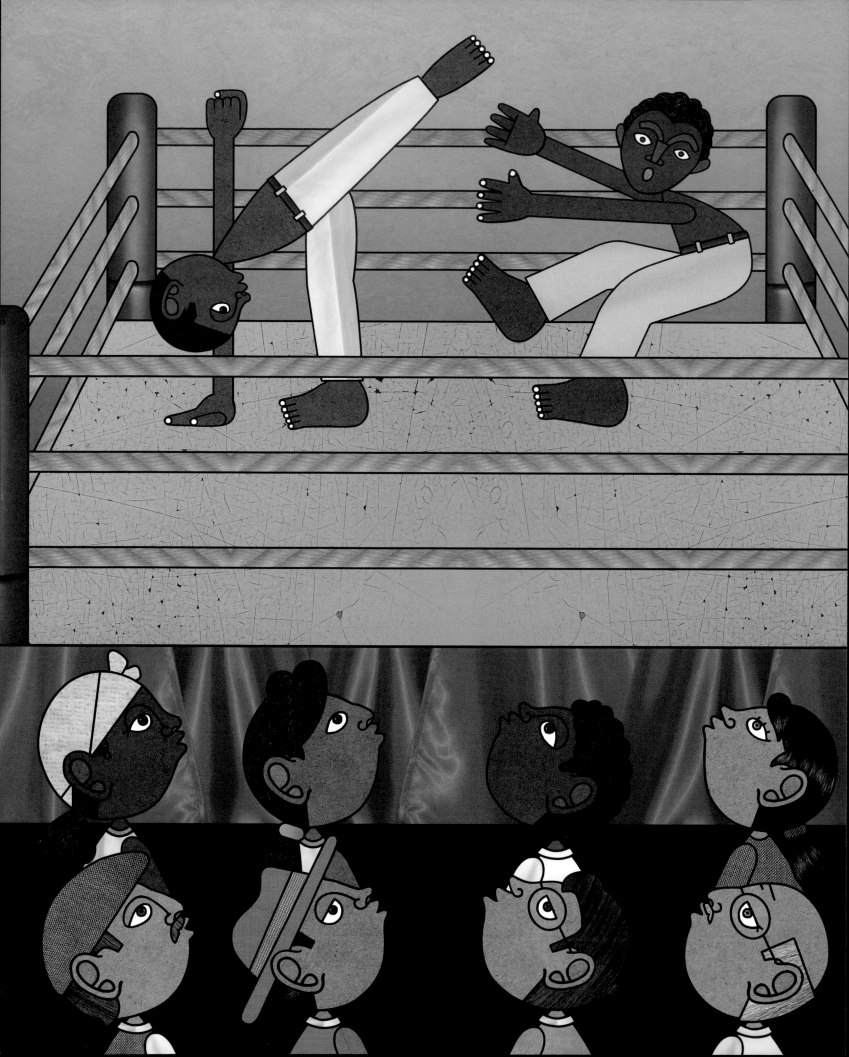

Between 1935 and 1936, several fighters responded to Bimba's challenge. The bouts took place at a newly inaugurated park. It was still illegal to practice capoeira in the streets, but because the fights took place inside a ring, the authorities let the mestre and other capoeiristas participate. The events were exciting. People bought tickets to see Mestre Bimba fight.

But the bouts were different from the capoeira that was usually played in a roda. There was no music, and the fighters tried to hit each other quickly. Bimba beat all his opponents with his powerful rabo de arraia kicks.

CAMPEÃO

The mestre was named Bahia's capoeira champion and his victories appeared in newspapers. Bimba was thrilled. He had proved that capoeira could be an effective fighting technique, but he was at a crossroads. Should capoeira become a sport to be practiced in the ring? Or should it remain a game to be played in a roda?

It did not take long for the mestre to make up his mind. Capoeira for him was more than fighting. It was also musical, and Bimba was a skilled and innovative berimbau player.

The game was also a celebration of his Bahian culture. Capoeira songs and stories often spoke of the history of Black people in Brazil and their resistance toward the oppression they experienced. The mestre didn't want those aspects of the jogo to be lost. "Capoeira," he said to his students, "is not for the ring. It is for life."

Bimba's academy and fights in the ring made capoeira popular among new sectors of the population. The government that was now in power was more tolerant of Black cultural expressions. In 1937, the mestre's efforts paid off and his school was officially recognized by the city's authorities.

In the following years, other mestres opened their own academies and developed their visions of the jogo. Capoeira in Bahia flourished, and it became an art that the different people of Salvador, especially Black people, could be proud of.

In the 1940s, Bimba's popularity, and that of other Bahian mestres, grew. Articles about Bimba kept appearing in newspapers. The persecution by the police that capoeiristas had experienced diminished. Capoeiristas from Salvador began to offer exhibits of the game. They often included other dances and Afro-Brazilian traditions in their shows.

They also began to travel and took the capoeira from Bahia to Rio de Janeiro, São Paulo, and other parts of Brazil.

Then, in 1953, a paramount moment occurred. Mestre Bimba and his students were invited to do an exhibit for the president of Brazil! President Getúlio Vargas was so impressed that he said, "Capoeira is the only truly national sport."

Soon after, the game was completely decriminalized. Capoeira was no longer illegal, and instead it became a Brazilian treasure.

Thanks to Bimba, other mestres, and their students, capoeira continued to spread. Women, who were rarely allowed to participate in the jogo before the 1960s, began to play it widely. Today, capoeira is played throughout Brazil and in more than 150 countries. The combination of fighting, dancing, music, acrobatics, and theatrics attracts people of all ages and social classes.

In 1974, Mestre Bimba passed away, but his life and accomplishments have been immortalized in many capoeira songs. He has achieved mythical status among players of the game. Mestre Bimba dedicated his whole being to capoeira, and while doing so, he helped turn a persecuted Afro-Brazilian cultural expression into a celebrated art practiced by millions around the world.

GLOSSARY

academia: (ah-kah-dem-ee-ah) academy or school.

aú: (ah-oo) an acrobatic move similar to a cartwheel.

axé: (ah-sheh) energy. The word comes from the Yoruba language.

batizado: (bah-tee-sad-oh) baptism.

batuque: (bah-too-keh) a now extinct Afro-Brazilian fighting game that was popular in Bahia. Bimba's father was a batuque champion. The game was played to music, and the objective was to knock one's opponent to the ground while they resisted.

berimbau: (bee-reem-bow) a percussion instrument that is shaped like a bow. The sound it produces comes from hitting the instrument's wire with a stick. A coin or rock is pressed against the wire to create different tones. A hollow gourd that is attached to the wooden bow and wire amplifies the sound. It is often played while holding a small, rattling instrument called caxixi (kah-shee-shee).

cabeçada: (kah-beh-sad-a) headbutt.

campeão: (kham-pea-ow) champion.

Candomblé: (khan-dom-bleh) an Afro-Brazilian religion. Candomblé honors the Orixás, which are deities that come from Yoruba religions in Africa. But the Orixás in Candomblé are also associated with Roman Catholic saints and holidays.

capoeira: (kah-poh-ey-rah) an athletic game played to music. The word "capoeira" has other meanings. It can refer to an area where trees and bushes are cut down for timber and agriculture. During Brazil's colonial period, enslaved people who ran away often had to cross open capoeiras to escape. Some linguists believe that the name for the athletic game is connected to this meaning of the word.

The word can also refer to a type of basket in which chickens and birds called capãos are kept. In the 1800s, the people who sold these birds were sometimes called capoeiras. Some researchers believe that the game of capoeira is related to this meaning of the word and that markets were among the first places the game was played.

ginga: (jean-gah) swing. This is the fundamental step in capoeira. It involves rocking back and forth and from side to side to the rhythm of the music.

jogo: (yo-go) game.

Luta Regional Baiana: (loo-tah reh-jee-oh-nal bah-ee-anna) a regional fight from Bahia. Some believe that Bimba called his style of capoeira "luta regional" in order to separate it from the stigma that the word "capoeira" carried at the time.

malandro: (mah-land-ro) thug. In capoeira, the word has been reclaimed and has assumed positive qualities. A player that is malandro or has malandragem is cunning or astute in the way they play the game.

meia lua: (meh-ee-ah loo-ah) literally "half-moon." A type of circular kick.

mestre: (mess-treh) teacher or master of a discipline. It is the highest level in capoeira.

pandeiro: (pan-day-roh) tambourine.

quilombo: (key-lum-boh) a community created by previously enslaved people. The Palmares quilombo was the biggest and most famous. It existed for most of the 1600s in what is now the state of Alagoas. At its height, it had close to thirty thousand inhabitants.

rabo de arraia: (rha-boh djee ah-rha-ee-ah) literally "stingray tail." A type of circular kick.

roda: (roh-dah) circle or wheel. Capoeiristas play the game inside a roda formed by other capoeiristas who sing, clap, and play percussion instruments.

samba: (sam-bah) a genre of music and dance. Samba has its origins in Bahia. It combines African and European musical traditions. The genre has evolved over time. It became especially popular in Rio de Janeiro in the twentieth century.

vingativa: (veen-gat-chee-bah) a move in which a player uses the torque of his shoulders and hips to knock his opponent to the ground.

AUTHOR'S NOTE

It is difficult to describe the art of capoeira to someone who has never experienced it. Capoeira can resemble a martial art, because it involves two people attacking and defending against each other with kicks and acrobatic moves. But capoeira, unlike many martial arts, is practiced to the sound of people singing, clapping, and playing percussion instruments like the pandeiro and the berimbau.

There are rarely winners or losers in capoeira. The players inside the roda, the circle of the game, are not really trying to hurt one another with their strikes, but instead show off their cunning and superior skills. Capoeiristas play *against* each other and *with* one another at the same time. The rhythm of the music determines how playful, confrontational, or collaborative the game is.

There are different stories that try to explain the game's origin. Some mestres have said that the jogo has its roots in Africa. In the Angola region, different tribes have practiced the n'golo, a ritual in which young men fight each other that has some similarities to capoeira.

In the 1500s, the Portuguese Empire began to trade enslaved people from different African nations. Portuguese slave traders took them by force to Brazil, their new colony in the Americas. Hundreds of African people would be packed into the holds of ships that would cross the Atlantic Ocean. It was a harrowing journey that lasted three months and thousands of Portuguese ships took part.

This inhumane practice lasted about three hundred years. Approximately four million African people were taken to Brazil. Hundreds of thousands died along the way. The African people who arrived in the new land did not bring with them any belongings, but they did bring their beliefs and their customs. Some capoeiristas believe that one of these customs was the n'golo ritual, which over time evolved into capoeira.

Other players and mestres say that the game originated in Brazil, not in Africa, and that it was developed by enslaved people who escaped the plantations, where they had been forced to farm sugarcane and other crops. After they escaped, many previously enslaved people created their own communities in the jungle called quilombos. Some capoeiristas say the game was born there as

Mestre Bimba, creator of capoeira regional (date unknown).

an expression of their freedom through music and movement. The plantation owners often attacked these communities and tried to recapture the people they claimed to have owned. But the quilombos resisted. Some players say capoeira was used there as a form of self-defense.

These origin stories have become part of the identity of capoeira, but the lack of concrete historical evidence makes it hard to know how true they are. Still, it is undeniable that capoeira is deeply connected to the history of Black people in Brazil. The earliest historical documents that mention capoeira are from the 1800s. They show that the game was played in port cities like Salvador and Rio de Janeiro, where the majority of people were descendants of enslaved people. Some historians believe that capoeira was born in these urban centers and that it began as a game that men played during their spare time or while they looked for work in the markets and on the docks.

Researchers are still discovering information about

Jogo da Capoeira by Johann Moritz Rugendas (1825) shows people of African descent in Brazil moving to the sound of music. Scholars believe that this is one of the earliest visual depictions of the capoeira game.

Two players accompanied by a berimbau and an atabaque.

and piecing together the history of the jogo. At times, it was tolerated by the authorities, but in 1890, two years after the abolition of slavery in Brazil, the game was prohibited throughout the nation. Capoeiristas were viciously persecuted by the authorities. It was unclear if the game would survive.

Manoel dos Reis Machado, better known as Bimba, was born in 1899 in the city of Salvador in Bahia. He became a major and transformative figure in capoeira. Bimba's talent for teaching the game and making it popular with new segments of Salvador's population helped usher in a new era for the jogo.

Bimba's efforts came at the right time. In the 1930s, Brazil's politicians and intellectuals had become interested in defining Brazil's national identity. They wanted to determine what aspects of life were uniquely Brazilian, and they grew more tolerant of Afro-Brazilian cultural expression. The first decades of the twentieth century were also a time when the government was interested in sports and martial arts as a way to improve its army.

During his life, Bimba became a hero to the people of Salvador, but not all Bahian capoeiristas agreed with

his vision for the game, which he called Luta Regional Baiana, or "regional" for short. In the late 1930s, a different school, capoeira Angola, was formed. The proponents of the Angola style emphasized the playful aspect of the game and its African roots. Angola was eventually led by Vicente Ferreira Pastinha, better known as Mestre Pastinha. Pastinha was a charismatic figure, and his style of capoeira was especially celebrated by Bahian artists and intellectuals. Contemporary capoeira, the kind that is practiced by many capoeiristas around the world today, evolved from both of these major styles.

While he was alive, Mestre Bimba saw capoeira flourish and grow. Sadly, despite his popularity, Mestre Bimba had financial difficulties. At the age of seventy-three, he decided to move to the city of Goiânia, where a student of his told him he could find good opportunities to teach capoeira. This turned out to be false. A year after he moved, Mestre Bimba suffered a stroke and died in poverty. His students and friends went to great lengths to bring his remains back to Bahia, where

Two players accompanied by a berimbau and a pandeiro.

they believed he belonged. His epitaph reads, "o rei da capoeira" (the king of capoeira).

In 2014, capoeira was declared an intangible cultural heritage of humanity by the United Nations Educational, Scientific and Cultural Organization (UNESCO). UNESCO awarded capoeira that distinction because the game promotes social integration and the memory of resistance to historical oppression.

I've been playing capoeira for several years. I feel lucky that I can bring my passion for making picture books and my passion for the jogo together in *Game of Freedom*. I wish to introduce the art of capoeira to children who are not familiar with the game and to honor one of its greatest legends. Axé!

Children play capoeira to the sound of the berimbau.

ENDNOTES

"They chase us like dogs." Alves de Almeida, *Bimba: perfil do mestre*, 14.

  Original quote: "The police chased capoeiristas as if they were chasing a crazy dog."

"Capoeira doesn't exist . . ." Alves de Almeida, *Bimba: perfil do mestre*, 27.

"Capoeira . . ." Assunção, *Capoeira: The History of an Afro-Brazilian Martial Art*, 131.

  Original quote: "Regional is not a fight for the ring, but for any situation in real life."

"Capoeira is the only truly national sport." Assunção, *Capoeira: The History of an Afro-Brazilian Martial Art*, 137.

BIBLIOGRAPHY

Abreu, Frederico José de. *Bimba é bamba: a capoeira no ringue*. Salvador, Brazil: Instituto Jair Moura, 1999.

Almeida, Bira. *Capoeira: A Brazilian Art Form*. Berkeley, CA: Blue Snake Books, 1986.

Alves de Almeida, Raimundo Cesar (Mestre Itapoan). *Bimba: perfil do mestre*. Salvador, Brazil: CED-UFBA, 1982.

Assunção, Matthias Röhrig. *Capoeira: The History of an Afro-Brazilian Martial Art*. New York: Taylor & Francis, 2005.

Campos, Hellio (Mestre Xaréu). *Capoeira Regional: a escola de Mestre Bimba*. Salvador, Brazil: EDUFBA, 2009.

Contemporary Capoeira. See capoeirahistory.com

Goulart, Luiz Fernando. *Mestre Bimba: A Capoeira Iluminada*. Rio de Janeiro: Lumen Produçoes, 2005.

Instituto do Patrimônio Histórico e Artístico Nacional. *Roda de Capoeira e Ofício dos Mestres de Capoeira*. Brasília: Iphan, 2014. (portal.iphan.gov.br/uploads/publicacao/DossieCapoeiraWeb.pdf)

Tour capoeirístico virtual da Bahia. *Mapa da Capoeira*. See mapadacapoeira.com.br

UNESCO. *Capoeira circle*. See ich.unesco.org/en/RL/capoeira-circle-00892